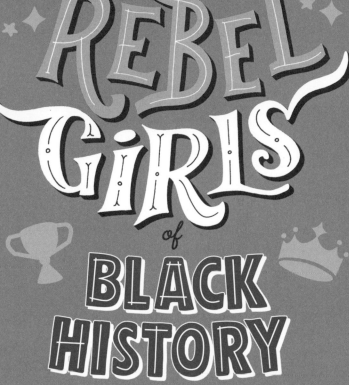

REBEL GIRLS

of

BLACK HISTORY

A Sticker-by-Number Book

DIAL BOOKS FOR YOUNG READERS

Dial Books for Young Readers
An imprint of Penguin Random House LLC, New York

First published in the United States of America by Dial Books for Young Readers,
an imprint of Penguin Random House LLC, 2021

Manufactured in China
ISBN 9780593407417

10 9 8 7 6 5 4 3 2 1
TOPL

Design by Jennifer Kelly and Cerise Steel
Text set in Montserrat and Woolwich

The publisher does not have any control over and does not assume
any responsibility for author or third-party websites or their content.

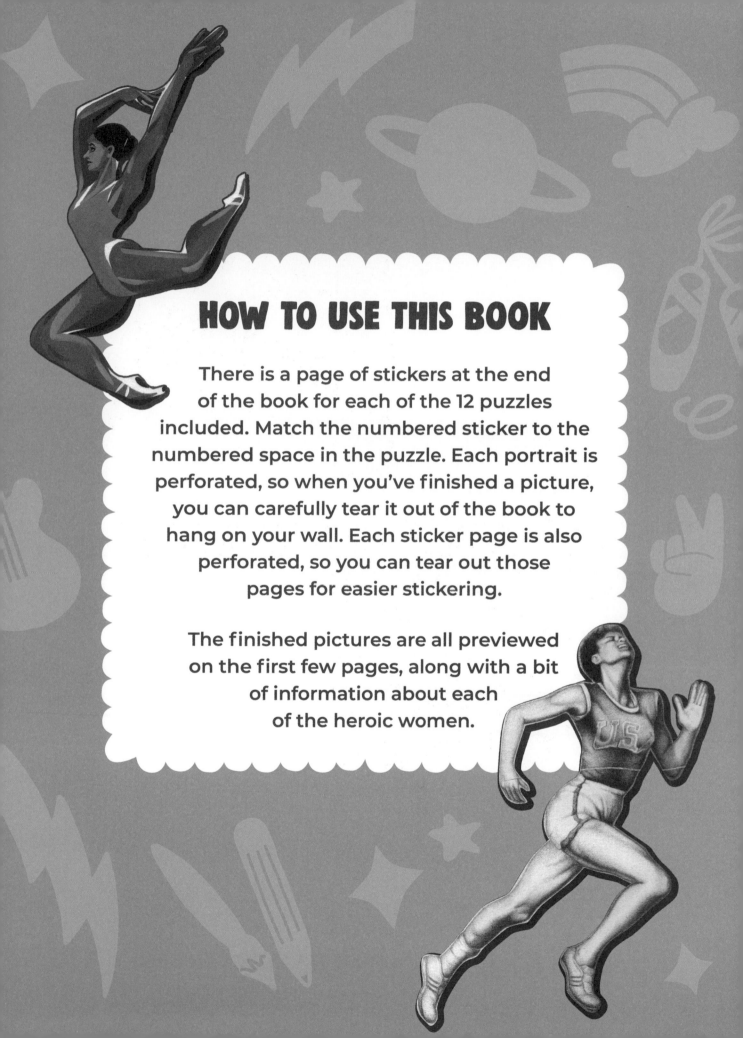

HOW TO USE THIS BOOK

There is a page of stickers at the end of the book for each of the 12 puzzles included. Match the numbered sticker to the numbered space in the puzzle. Each portrait is perforated, so when you've finished a picture, you can carefully tear it out of the book to hang on your wall. Each sticker page is also perforated, so you can tear out those pages for easier stickering.

The finished pictures are all previewed on the first few pages, along with a bit of information about each of the heroic women.

Madam C. J. Walker
Businesswoman
December 23, 1867–May 25, 1919

Madam C. J. Walker was the first female self-made millionaire in the United States. Born a few years after the Emancipation Proclamation, she was the only girl in her family who had never been enslaved. As a young woman, she was upset that none of the hair products available were right for Black people's hair. So she created her own hair care line. The products were very much needed, and soon Madam C. J. Walker was a success nationwide.

Illustration by Cristina Spanò

Harriet Tubman
Freedom Fighter
c. 1822–March 10, 1913

Harriet Tubman spent her entire life bravely fighting for the freedom of others. Born into a life of slavery, she succeeded in escaping when she was just a teenager. She returned to the South over and over again to rescue other enslaved people, first via the Underground Railroad network of activists, and then as a Union scout during the Civil War. By the time slavery was outlawed in the United States, Harriet had rescued hundreds of people.

Illustration by Sally Nixon

Ida B. Wells
Journalist and Activist
July 16, 1862–March 25, 1931

Ida B. Wells was one of the most influential writers and speakers of the early civil rights and women's rights movements. She helped found the National Association for the Advancement of Colored People (NAACP), as well as several organizations for women. And as a journalist, she bravely documented serious crimes that were being committed against Black people in the United States. After her death, she was awarded a Pulitzer Prize for her "outstanding and courageous reporting."

Illustration by Adriana Bellet

Kamala Harris
Vice President
Born October 20, 1964

This groundbreaking attorney and politician is the first female, first Black, and first South Asian vice president of the United States. She took office in January 2021 alongside President Joe Biden. Before that, Kamala Harris graduated from Howard University and Hastings College of the Law, became a district attorney, served as the attorney general of California, and spent an influential term as a United States senator.

Illustration by Nicole Miles

Katherine Johnson, Dorothy Vaughan, and Mary Jackson
Computer Scientists

Katherine Johnson, August 26, 1918–February 24, 2020
Dorothy Vaughan, September 20, 1910–November 10, 2008
Mary Jackson, April 9, 1921–February 11, 2005

These three women were brilliant scientists who worked for NASA, finding answers to complex math problems that would make space travel safe. Katherine was the only person astronaut John Glenn trusted to verify important calculations. Dorothy was the first person to figure out how to use an IBM transistor-based computer for NASA's work. And Mary was the first Black female aeronautical engineer, specializing in the behavior of air around planes. Today they are celebrated as three of the most inspiring people in the history of space travel.

Illustration by Cristina Portolano

Misty Copeland
Ballet Dancer

Born September 10, 1982

Misty Copeland was a dance prodigy from the age of 13, when she began learning ballet. In 2015, she became the first Black woman to be a principal dancer with American Ballet Theatre, one of the most prestigious ballet companies in the world.

Illustration by Ping Zhu

Nina Simone
Musician
February 21, 1933–April 21, 2003

Nina Simone learned to play her first song on the piano at the age of three. As a child, she trained as a classical pianist. As an adult, her focus turned to pop, gospel, and jazz. She became known and admired not only for her musical skill but also for the civil rights content of her songs. One of the most influential singers and activists in the United States, she was inducted into the Rock & Roll Hall of Fame a few years after her death.

Illustration by T. S. Abe

Oprah Winfrey
Media Superstar and Philanthropist
Born January 29, 1954

From childhood on, Oprah Winfrey loved to talk, and her speaking skills led to her first jobs, on radio and in TV news. But Oprah's true calling was as a talk show host. She listened deeply to her guests, and she always understood their pain and joy. After launching her own TV program nationwide, she became the queen of talk shows. Eventually, she took on acting and magazine publishing and founded her own network. A multi-billionaire, she is one of the most generous philanthropists in the world.

Illustration by T. S. Abe

Ruby Bridges
Activist
Born September 8, 1954

Ruby Bridges was just six years old when she became the first Black student to attend the all-white school near her home. Even though it was illegal to refuse to admit Black students based on the color of their skin, her town didn't want to admit it. She needed to be accompanied by United States marshals to keep her safe as she walked to and from that school. Ruby's bravery opened the doors to equal and inclusive education for all Black students in the nation.

Illustration by Giulia Tomai

Serena and Venus Williams
Tennis Champions
Serena, born September 26, 1981
Venus, born June 17, 1980

Sisters Serena and Venus Williams started playing tennis as preschoolers, and their talents were quickly apparent. Both of them played their first professional tournaments at the age of 14. It wasn't long before each sister had been ranked #1 in the world by the Women's Tennis Association, winning numerous Grand Slams, the most prestigious of all tennis championships. As a doubles team, they have won 14 Grand Slam titles!

Illustration by Debora Guidi

Sojourner Truth
Activist
c. 1797–November 26, 1883

Isabella Baumfree was enslaved until the age of 29, when she escaped with her baby daughter. Soon after, she went to court to fight for her son Peter's freedom, and she won!—the first Black woman to win a court case against a white man. Later she would change her name to Sojourner (meaning "traveler") Truth and spend the rest of her life criss-crossing the states as a speaker, advocating for women's rights and the abolition of slavery.

Illustration by Cristina Amodeo

Wilma Rudolph
Athlete
June 23, 1940–November 12, 1994

When Wilma Rudolph was a young child, the polio vaccine had not yet been discovered. She contracted the terrible illness and was left with a paralyzed leg. Her doctor said she might never walk again, but her mother refused to give up and took her to weekly treatments. By the time she was nine, Wilma could walk again. By the time she was 20, she had become the fastest woman in the world, breaking three running records at the Olympic Games.

Illustration by Alice Barberini

MADAM C. J. WALKER

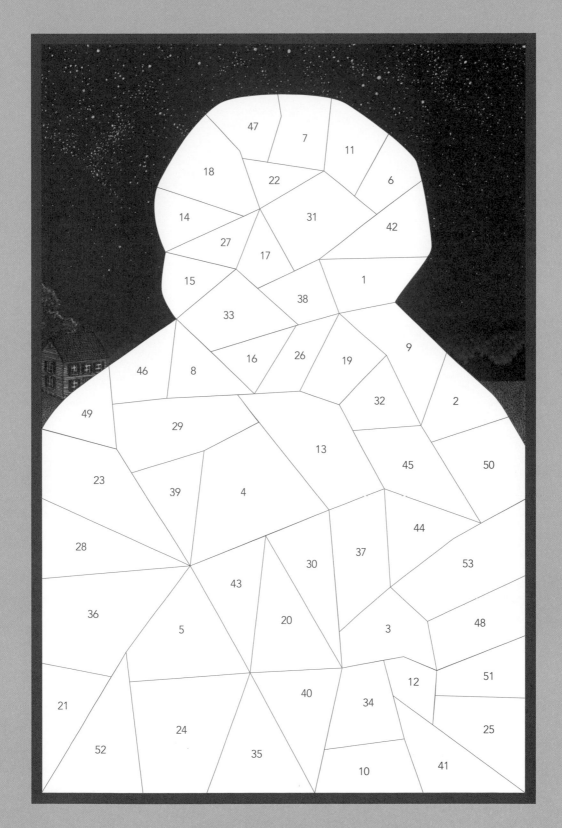

HARRIET TUBMAN

IDA B. WELLS

KAMALA HARRIS

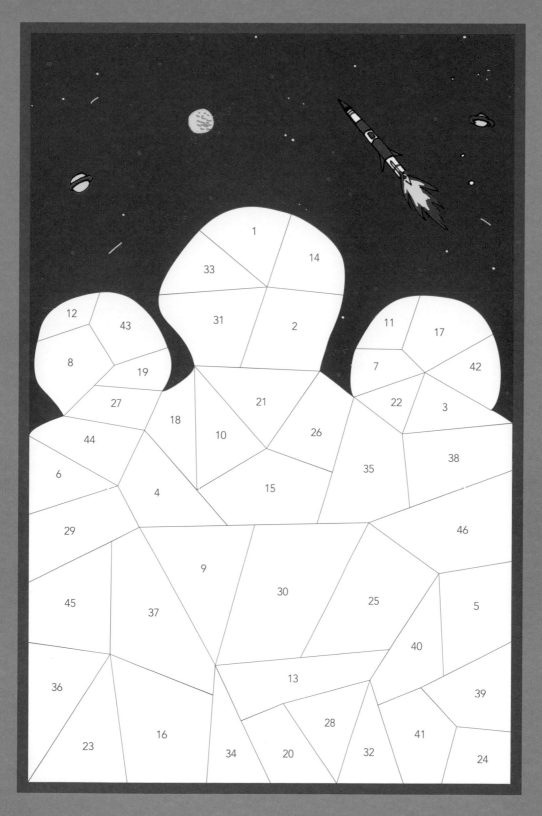

KATHERINE JOHNSON, DOROTHY VAUGHAN,
AND MARY JACKSON